The White Angel

The White Angel

Angel

The Memoirs of Vincent
Conlan

Sara Downing

ISBN-13: 9781072352143

To Us A Son Is Given

There's a lady here. She wants to take one of us home with her.

She keeps looking at Rose with a funny little smile, so I don't think it's going to be me. Rose is still a baby, and she's been here since she was born. She's really small, still in a cot, even though she can toddle about on her own now, all chubby and wobbly.

Everyone's little here, except for me. I'm a big boy. The biggest boy. I'm six, now, so I'm really grown up compared to all the babies that live here. They're a noisy lot, crying all the time. I don't make a din like they do, but even though I'm much bigger than they are the nuns still make me eat the same old mushy food as them. I think mush must be the only thing they know how to cook. It gets a bit boring. And it tastes yucky. All the flavours are mixed in together, but then it doesn't really taste of anything much at all.

She's pretty, though, Rose. That's probably why they want her. A bonny little girl, all of their own, to go and live with them *somewhere in a nice house. In a proper house, not a place like this, with her own Mummy and Daddy. Perhaps they'll get her a pet — a dog or a cat, something furry to cuddle up to at night. And maybe she'll have a brother or a sister. Someone to play with who is your own and just yours. Someone you can belong to. Here we all belong to everyone and no one, all at once.*

She looks nice, I think, this lady. Smart, with a hat, and a fancy bag hanging over her arm with a shiny clasp, and shiny shoes with bows on them. She's come here with another lady, and I've seen that one before. She's called Mrs Shepherd and she works for the Social, Matron says. I don't know what that means, the Social, but whenever she arrives, another one of us always comes, or someone goes. We never know which way it's going to be till it happens.

Today Mrs Shepherd brought this lady with her, the one with the hat and the bag, so that she can choose a child. One to take home, to keep. And she's taking Rose. She doesn't want someone like me, someone they just call Boy. She wants a child with a real name. A Rose. A child you want to keep has to have a real name all of their own.

I watch as the lady bends down. She puts her bag on the floor and looks at Rose.

'Hello, Rose,' she says, and her eyes twinkle like the pretty ring on her finger. She has nice clothes and nice things and she looks how a mummy should look. Like a mummy in a picture book. 'My name is Barbara and I'd really like it if you could come and live with me.' She smiles at Rose, but Rose doesn't smile back.

Rose is too little to understand. Even I know that you don't talk to babies in that way. Rose just stands there and looks down at her tatty little booties. Maybe the lady will give her some shiny shoes too, if she becomes her mummy. A little pair of shiny shoes with sparkly buckles, not old and worn out ones that come from a box of mixed up shoes. Shoes that she's paid real money for, in a proper shoe shop.

Mrs Shepherd says: 'Come on, Rose, say hello to Mrs Smith.' Rose doesn't know how to say hello to people yet. She still blabbers like a baby, because she is a baby. Mrs Shepherd puts her finger under Rose's chin and tries to make her look up.

'Well, Rose, you are going to come and live with me!' says this Barbara lady, standing up again. She doesn't seem to mind that Rose looks a bit sad and confused. Then Mrs Shepherd touches her arm and pulls her to one side. I can see them pointing at me as they talk.

'Just for a few weeks, that's all it would be,' I hear Mrs Shepherd say. They think I can't hear them, but they're whispering really loudly. 'Just until we can find a more permanent solution for him. He's getting too old to stay here now, with all these babies. It isn't good for him.'

'Well...' Barbara says. She gives me a right old look up and down then, like she's trying to work out if I'm a good boy or not. I don't say anything. I never say anything.

I'd really like to go with her, to get away from this place, but I try not to get too excited. It's happened like this before, and three times I went to stay with someone, but then I've always come back again. Normally they want babies, you see, or little toddlers with cute, round faces and curly hair, like Rose. No one wants a silent six year old with sad eyes to go and live with them. Where's the fun in that?

They go all quiet and then they talk a bit more and finally Mrs Shepherd comes over to me. She doesn't really explain what's happening, but before I know it, I'm fetching my things and I'm in the car with them.

It's a miracle! It really happened and the lady, Barbara, is taking me home with her! I can't believe it. I'm finally going to have a mummy and daddy all of my own, and little Rose as my sister. I'd have preferred a brother, obviously, but she'll do, even though she's a bit small to be much fun at the moment. When she's bigger, she'll be alright to play with. Better than no one, anyway.

The car smells all lovely. Clean and polished. I sniff it up like it's the smell of freedom. I can't get enough of it. I sit there with my legs dangling and I look around me at the lovely smooth, cool seats, and stroke my hand across them. I can't stop smiling. Being here is like a miracle, it really is. Nothing this good normally happens to me. I want to pinch myself to make sure I'm not dreaming.

This is the beginning of something amazing for me, I know it is. My new life is about to start.

In The Beginning

My name is Vincent Conlan and this is the story of my early years.

Every adult is shaped by childhood experiences, and this book is my way of explaining how and why I'm the person I am today. For all the positive things that have happened to me, it's a way of saying thank you to those who have helped me. And for the not so good things, well, I'd like to hope that lessons can be learned from them. Every child deserves a chance in life.

Some of the tales I will now go on to tell have come to light recently, pieced together from information I have found, and records which I have been able to unearth. This hasn't been an easy task, to say the least. Since I founded the Croome Court School page on Facebook more has come to light, and sharing experiences with former classmates and friends has helped us all to remember more, and support one another in our discoveries. Now we have a reunion at Croome every year, and this has been a revelation for us all.

I was born out of wedlock on 1st April 1955 to a Catholic mother, Elizabeth. She was brought up in a small town in County Cork, Southern Ireland. It was a close-knit community, with very traditional Catholic values, and the whole family was deeply religious. Elizabeth's uncle was Father Doyle, the local parish priest. He was a frequent visitor to the family home, forever popping in to see everyone, a real character, apparently. His sister, my mother's aunt, took holy orders and went to live in Australia as Sister Columbia.

In her late teens my mother moved to London and went into domestic service, where she met Michael, the man who would later become my father. He was also Irish, and I believe he was a builder. For a couple of years the pair of them were blissfully happy, and then Elizabeth fell pregnant. Imagining that they would marry quickly, in plenty of time for him to make an 'honest woman' of her, Elizabeth broke the news to him. His reaction couldn't have been further from her expectations. Instead of delight at his forthcoming fatherhood, the joy of having a child with the woman he loved, he told her that she needed to get rid of the baby.

Elizabeth was horrified. She could never contemplate an abortion – which in any case was illegal

– and so she and Michael parted ways, with him leaving both her and London and moving to Birmingham. A heartbroken Elizabeth remained in London, sending him a constant stream of letters, begging him to change his mind. Throughout the pregnancy she still harboured dreams of the two of them being reconciled and raising their baby together.

Her attempts at a reconciliation were futile, and in March 1955 my mother found herself in the Crusade of Rescue Centre in Highbury (now the Catholic Children's Society). This home was established in the twenties and could accommodate up to twelve Roman Catholic girls between the ages of 17 and 26, who were expecting or had just had, their first child, and found themselves in difficulties. After the birth, the women would be expected to stay and work at the home for several months, caring for their own child and the other children who lived there.

In Ireland, women were expected to remain in such homes for up to two years, but in England it was usually just a few months, and so I would like to think that my mother had a better time of it, falling pregnant in England rather than Ireland. Back there, she would most likely have been cast out by her religious family, who wouldn't have been able to bear the scandal brought upon them by having an unmarried mother in their midst. However, even in England, it was still a couple of decades before having a child out of wedlock would become socially acceptable. These poor women were considered immoral and their children a drain on resources. I can't begin to imagine the shame my mother must have felt.

And so, in inauspicious circumstances, baby Vincent came into the world. Despite Elizabeth's constant pleas, Michael did not come to visit us even once.

During that era many Irish Catholic organisations feared that Irish babies born in England might be adopted into Protestant families. Generally the Irish authorities would try to persuade the women to come back to Ireland with the child, into a Catholic mother-and-baby home. One organisation, the Catholic Protection and Rescue Society of Ireland assisted the repatriation of 2,600 unmarried mothers. After the discovery in recent years of so many atrocities at these mother-and-baby homes, I can only be thankful now that the two of us weren't sent to one of them.

During my investigations it came to light that my mother's application for repatriation wasn't for herself and me, however, but for me alone. What she wanted was to send me back home to Ireland, but stay in England herself, and so I was put on an adoption list of bastard children born to Catholic women in the UK.

As a parent and a grandparent now, I can't begin to imagine how someone – particularly a mother – could contemplate separation from their child, especially one so young. I've often liked to think that the decision to send me home alone was the hardest one my mother would ever have had to make, knowing that she would never see me again. Sadly I don't believe this was the case; I think she still harboured some kind of misplaced hope that, unencumbered by a small child, and remaining in England as a single woman again, she might have another chance at a relationship with Michael. She put her own needs and desires way ahead of her child's.

I would lay down my life for my own family, and do anything to be with them. I can't imagine ever letting my reputation and standing within the community overshadow those feelings. I know things were different back in those days, and how shameful it was to conceive a child out of wedlock, particularly in the Catholic faith, and so I feel no hatred towards my mother for what she did. But if it were me, I would have fought to stay with my child. The wrong in all of this isn't bringing the child into the world, but in abandoning that child to an uncertain future.

As an innocent baby I was nothing more than a burden around my mother's neck.

When I reached adulthood I did wonder for many years why my mother hadn't left some kind of trail that I could follow later in life, so that I could track her down. At the time it probably didn't occur to her to do something like that, and if she wanted to reignite her relationship with my father, chances are it was far from her mind. But I can't help wondering if she ever gave any consideration to how I would feel once I grew up.

If she didn't want a relationship with me as a child, couldn't we reconnect and have one later in life?

The only correspondence I have ever seen from my mother are her letters to the authorities, begging them to take me for adoption. It's very sad to have this as the only written record of her. For many years I couldn't help but wonder if she ever told the man she eventually went on to marry that she already had a child, and that she had deserted him. For a while I considered that I might have some half-brothers and - sisters somewhere in the world, and then recently I discovered that in fact I do – one half-brother and two half-sisters. Until I made contact with them, they were completely unaware of my existence. A new relative suddenly appearing out of the blue can cause a lot of disquiet within a family, but it's so much easier to trace people these days, with the internet and various ancestry and DNA websites, so I'm sure it must happen a lot.

More recently I have found out that my mother married in the late 1950s. Apparently she told her husband about the child she had left behind. When I was twelve or thirteen the family decided to return to Ireland and he told her to go and find the son she had given up and bring him back to Ireland with them. My mother then asked one of her brothers to approach Norwich council children's department to find where I was. It does seem that the authorities had every intention of tracking me down and reuniting me

10

with my family, however Norwich council could not locate my file and therefore it was presumed that I had died. As far as they were concerned, if there was no file then there was no child. What a tragedy that was for me, a missed opportunity to have a whole new chance at life with my real family. I believe now that this is why my mother didn't tell her other children about me. Perhaps she was ashamed of what she had done, and gave some thought to how all of our lives could have been so different. None more so than for me.

My youngest half-sister told me about this recently. When we met for the first time she suggested that I take a DNA test, and when it was confirmed that I was Elizabeth's son it put their minds at rest. I think they must have found it hard to reconcile the kind mother they knew with the one who had abandoned a child, and there is no doubt that it would have been easier for them if the DNA test had proved negative and I disappeared from their lives again.

But from the moment I traced her, my mother never doubted that I was her son. My half-sister said she used to go very quiet around the time of my birthday each year, almost as though she was in mourning. Clearly she hadn't forgotten about me completely. Elizabeth had been a wonderful mother, kind and protective. It must have been so hard for them all to come to terms with my appearance, but since finding out about me I believe they all understand her a little better. And for me, it's wonderful to have discovered this new family of mine, and I am glad to feel that I am fully a part of their lives now.

If I'd met with my mother earlier in my adulthood I knew I could have found it in my heart to forgive her for what she did. I didn't blame her, but instead I directed my anger towards the Catholic doctrine for the power it exerted over unmarried mothers. Once we had been reunited I didn't want my mother to carry the scar of what she had done. When I held her in my arms for the last time, as we said goodbye and she saw me off on the plane back to England, I'm sure I could feel that pain leave her body. I knew she felt as complete at that moment as I did.

I do still blame the Church for what happened to a certain extent. I believe in God, but my faith in the Catholic Church is nowhere near as strong as the love I feel for God. They are two separate entities, and for me, the Church itself is still on trial.

An Eye for an Eye

Whilst the repatriation application was in progress, I developed a twitch in one eye. At this point I was about eight months old. My mother took me to Great Ormond Street hospital, where the doctors informed her that it was probably a result of me being educationally subnormal.

It's shocking, now, to hear the word used to describe me – a retard. I didn't uncover this story until I was in my fifties and thank heavens it's not a word we use any more. In this day and age I feel we have more respect for human beings, no matter what ails them.

The authorities also blamed my condition on lack of physical and emotional contact as a result of my upbringing, and asked that I be brought back again in a few weeks' time for assessment. My mother was worried that if something was found to be wrong with me, then I might be excluded from the repatriation programme, so she refused to take me back there. I can imagine that she thought my being labelled a 'retard' would be enough to scupper her chances of packing me back off to Ireland and carrying on with her life in London. As far as she was concerned, the doctor had misdiagnosed my condition and so, casting medical opinion aside, she sought instead the help of her local priest to support her in her attempts to send me back to Ireland.

My mother's worst fears were realised when I was rejected from the adoption programme. Around the same time as this she heard that her aunt, Sister Columbia, was due to return to Ireland to visit the family, and my mother was summoned home to attend the reunion.

My mother hadn't even told her family of her pregnancy, let alone that she now had a baby son, and so returning to Ireland was the last thing she wanted to do. She couldn't risk her secret getting out, and ran as far east in England as she possibly could, ending up near Great Yarmouth. There she deposited me in a private nursing home and returned to London.

To begin with my mother would send money to the nursing home, but it wasn't long before the payments began to dry up. Despite the nursing home's best efforts, no one was able to trace her, and when the police were called in, they were also unsuccessful. She had succeeded in disappearing from my life.

I was sent to Norwich hospital, where again that dreadful tag – retard – was applied to me. When I look back from my position of relative comfort in life now, I can't imagine how anyone could be so cruel as to condemn a small child to a doomed life on the basis of a misdiagnosis and that dreadful word. Despite everyone's low expectations of me, apparently I made great progress in that hospital and they would have been quite happy to release me, if only I'd had somewhere to go.

Whilst I was away from the nursing home one of the carers made it her mission to make contact with my mother. She had a kind heart, and her main concern was to reunite me with my mother, so that I could have some chance at a normal family life.

Aside from that, it's fair to say that the authorities in charge of the home would have quite liked to absolve themselves from any responsibility for me, and so the search for my mother was threefold, driven by the desire to have me off their hands, to have some recompense for the care they had provided thus far, but also to reunite a child with his mother.

My treatment at the hospital stalled when it turned out that parental consent was needed; with no traceable relative, they came to the decision that there was nothing more they could do for me, and so I was discharged.

Once again I was an unwanted child, and once again I was shipped off, ending up at a convent just outside

Great Yarmouth. That was the defining moment from which all ties of any kind with my family were severed.

As a small child aged just six, I was now utterly alone in the world. It was from this convent that Barbara was persuaded to take me home with her, and off I went to begin the next chapter in my life, ever hopeful that this time there would be a change for the better.

An Epiphany

I'm not going to be staying with Barbara for long. But that's fine, because I'm just happy to be away from the convent and all those tiny babies and the noise they make.

They soon realise that I'm a bit slow, Barbara and her husband. He's called Stan. I don't pick things up very quickly. Someone told them I was a retard, but I'm not, and they know that. I just haven't done things that a lot of boys my age have done, so I don't know what to do. That's not my fault. I can't help it. Maybe now I'll start to catch up and I'll soon be as smart as all the other children at my school.

'Come and have your tea,' Barbara says to me, so I do as I'm told and I go and sit at the table. My tummy is rumbling. I look at what's on my plate but I don't know what it is.

'Eat up, then,' says Stan, as I sit there, not knowing what to do. I look for a spoon, but there's only a fork and a knife and I don't know how to use them.

'Use your fork,' says Barbara. 'Like this.' She shows me what to do and I copy her.

I stab the sausage with my fork and I nibble at the end of it. It's really nice, but it catches in the back of my throat and makes me gag. I cough so much that I have to go out of the room. I go into the toilet and all of the food in my mouth goes down the pan.

'He's being sick again,' I can hear Barbara saying. 'It's not right, is it? There must be something wrong with him. All little boys like sausages, don't they?' She lets out a big sigh.

I like the taste of Barbara's food so much, but I don't know what to do with it when it's in my mouth. It seems to get stuck and then that really hurts my chest and I have to go to the toilet and get rid of it. I'm so hungry but I just can't eat anything she cooks for me, and that makes her cross. I think it must be because of all the soft food at the convent. Everything we ate there was soft and we didn't have to chew. We just spooned it in, all soft and gooey, and down the hatch it went.

'What are we going to do with you?' Barbara says when I come back to the table. I put my fork into some of the mash, and that goes down alright, because it's nice and soft. It's just things like that juicy, tasty sausage that I can't eat. My body just doesn't like it, even though my tongue loves the taste.

'Come on, Vincent,' Barbara says now. 'Let's take you upstairs for your bath.' I just sit still. I don't know who Vincent is. She keeps saying this word to me, as if I should know who Vincent is, but I don't. In the convent they just called me Boy, or You. Vincent's not my name, is it? It's a real person's name, not a name for a boy like me.

She takes me by the hand and leads me up the stairs. I sit on the bathroom floor and she puts some water into the bath.

'Vincent is your name,' she says. But I still don't believe her. Someone like me doesn't have a real name.

One day Barbara says: *'Vincent, I'm taking you to see the dentist. I think there must be a problem with your teeth, and that's why you can't eat.'*

I want to tell her that it's not my teeth, it's her food, but I decide not to as I know she'd think that was rude. So I go along to the dentist with her, and I sit in the special chair.

'We are going to take out all of your baby teeth,' the dentist says. 'Then you will be able to eat properly.'

I don't know what it means, taking teeth out, or how they do it or how it feels, but there's nothing I can do or say. I just have to let them do it, so that's what happens. There's a lot of blood and my mouth is really sore for days afterwards. When my gums heal up and stop bleeding, I can see that there are some new, bigger teeth trying to push through. I really hope the dentist doesn't want to steal those out of my mouth, too.

Mrs Shepherd should have told Barbara about the food we ate at the convent but she didn't. Then I tried to tell Barbara, but she wouldn't listen. I think she thought I was being naughty, not eating her food. I don't think she really knows what to do with me. Rose is such a perfect little girl, always so good, and I'm the problem one, the one who makes her cross and gets in the way. It's always me.

Barbara doesn't really want me here, I know that. She only ever really wanted Rose. No one wants me.

'You're a burden on the state, Vincent', she tells me one day. I don't understand what that means, but it doesn't sound good.

Unto Us a Child is Born

Barbara hadn't really wanted me in the first place, and I'd already been in their home for much longer than I was meant to be. I had outstayed my welcome and she began to resent me.

I must have been around seven years old when she believed herself to be pregnant. She was over the moon and excitedly showing off to all her friends. Sadly, despite the symptoms she was presenting with, it was soon found to be a phantom pregnancy.

I'd like to believe that Barbara wasn't a bad woman, or intentionally unkind. She was just ill-equipped to deal with my needs, and not supported at all by the authorities, who were relieved to have me off their hands. She was also an incredibly proud woman, and when the pregnancy was found not to be a true pregnancy, this changed her personality. She became quite unstable, and was very bitter and twisted. It was quite a shock to see this sudden change in her.

When her disappointment about the failed pregnancy turned to anger, there was one obvious person she could take her frustrations out on – me. Some days she would hurt me, physically and mentally, hurling abuse as well as blows.

And then one day I was involved in a nasty accident. I was running late for school because I'd had some chores to do before leaving, so I had to run to catch the bus. In those days the buses had a platform at the back where you could jump on, and a pole to hang onto. The bus was already at the bus stop and I could see it was about to pull away so I jumped on quickly. I managed to get my left foot on, and my hand around the pole, however as the bus moved off my hand slipped down the pole and my right foot hit the ground. I couldn't let go because there was a big truck behind us and so I was dragged along for a while, with my foot stuck, until the conductor spotted me. He grabbed me by my collar and was able to pull me on board. A few days later my foot was so swollen that I couldn't put my shoe on. It was almost as though my index toe had been stretched. I can remember the pain of it to this day.

At the hospital they said that my toe had stretched so much that the tip would need to be removed to get it back to a normal length. I can't for one minute imagine that this is how such an injury would be treated in this day and age. Thinking back on it, it seems utterly barbaric.

After the operation I had to have my foot in a cast for six weeks, and as a seven year old boy, it was tough to know that I would have to rest for so long. Worse was still to come, as at this stage no one knew that I would have an allergic reaction to the plaster.

I can remember my relief on the day the plaster cast was finally to be removed, believing freedom was just around the corner. As they were removing the stitches the nurses noticed large blisters on my leg and all over my foot. But just as their concern for me was growing, there was a distraction across the room as a young girl was carried in, kicking and screaming. I don't know what was wrong with her, but it took five people to carry her in, and I remember finding the whole experience very traumatic.

When Barbara saw my distress she insisted that I was taken out of the room immediately. By then, only part of the stitches had been removed, and to this day the rest of them are still in my foot. For some reason I was never taken back to have them removed. Nowadays I still have very little feeling in that toe, and the remaining stitches stick up like small spikes, but oddly they don't really bother me. I don't know who was to blame for this failure, the hospital or Barbara. I've always liked to think that everyone was doing their best, but sometimes I really don't know if that was the case.

Once the cast was off, my leg had to be bandaged, and the dressings changed every evening. Given the blisters, this was excruciatingly painful. Barbara believed that the best course of treatment was to put a bowl of boiling water underneath my foot, so that the steam would penetrate the blisters and soak out the poison. Every day this terrifying experience would take place, and I grew to dread it. I would scream and cry and occasionally pass out with the pain of it. Sometimes I tried to hide, but I knew that I'd still have to have it done before the new bandages could be applied. It went on for weeks. Despite my screams of agony, I think Barbara believed she was doing the right thing by me. I do try to see the best in people, in spite of everything.

Barbara continued to struggle with depression following the phantom pregnancy, and although she seemed to love little Rose, and lavish attention on her, she grew to resent me even more. Then there came a time when I wasn't even allowed to play with Rose, her precious little girl.

Barbara realised she could hurt me and get away with it, and once she was in that mindset, my 'punishments' escalated, until one day there was an incident and my mistreatment came to the attention of someone else.

At school I would always make sure I changed for football with my back against the cabinets, away from the other boys, so that no one could see my injuries. It was my special trick, just to keep everything hidden. I thought it was easier if no one knew. One day, though, I became distracted, my trick didn't work so well, and a friend spotted the marks all over my back. He insisted on taking me to see his mother, and he made me show her my back. They lived in the shop next door to us, and although that made things awkward she went ahead and reported it to the authorities. My back was covered in cigarette burns and buckle marks. To this day I can't look at a belt buckle without a shiver running down my spine.

Barbara was reported on several occasions for mistreating me, but I continued to stay with her. There was nowhere else for me to go, plus she was a friend of Mrs Shepherd, the social worker who had placed me with her. Mrs Shepherd had once said to me that if I had any problems, I should go and see her at her office. But I never knew where that office was. I found out recently that it was in Norwich, a place I didn't even know existed when I was a child.

Despite being at the heart of a family which was supposed to be looking after me, once again I found myself alone.

The Lord Is My Shepherd

They've told me I need to have my own bedroom. I'm not allowed to share with Rose anymore. She's too precious, and I'm the spare part that they want to tidy away every night, out of sight and out of mind.

Part of me thinks I should be excited about having my own room. After all those years of sleeping in dormitories, the idea of a space to call my own ought to be brilliant, but it isn't. And that's because I know that they're doing this for themselves, not for me, and I realise this when they tell me where my new bedroom is going to be.

'You're going up there,' Barbara says to me one day, pointing up the second, narrow flight of stairs. 'That room, up in the attic, right at the top.' I'm not quite sure where she means, but I know I'll find out eventually.

I hide in a dark corner on the stairs and watch as the workmen come in. They traipse up and down, carrying ladders and tools, bits and bobs. There's a lot of bashing and banging for a while and then I stand out of the way, just along the landing, and watch as they bring down the big water tank from the boiler room. I don't understand why they're doing that, so I shoot up the stairs once they're all down and go for a look.

It's the tiniest room in the house, and there's a nasty, spidery space where the tank was. Lots of bare pipes and wires and it's not very cosy at all. This can't be my new bedroom, surely? It's not much more than a cupboard. And then Barbara comes up, and she's got a little bed for me, which she's putting up in there.

This is my new room, this tiny cupboard. I understand now.

'This is your new bedroom, Vincent,' she says. She's smiling, but there's something behind her eyes that didn't used to be there. When I first came to live here there was a spark in them, but they're different now. Flat-looking.

She's putting me in a cupboard. It's not even a bedroom, it's so tiny. I close the door and sit down on the bed. If I stretch my arms out I can touch both sides of the room at once, it's so small. If I stand up, there's only a little space by the door, and that's it.

There's no window, and the light switch is outside the room. I don't like it. I don't like it that the room can be locked from the outside and the light turned off and on from outside the door. It makes me feel scared, and all panicked inside. I run downstairs quickly, away from my new room. I don't like it in there.

I've been naughty today. Well, actually I haven't actually been naughty at all, but Barbara says I have. Naughty to her means that I've upset her. I've said something or done something she doesn't like, although for the life of me I can't think what it is this time.

27

'Go to your room, Vincent,' she yelled at me. 'You're making me exhausted. I can't cope with you now. I'll deal with you later, just you wait.'

So I've been sent up here. Up to my room. My tiny cupboard in the attic with no window. Not even sent, really. Today she dragged me up here, pushed me inside and locked the door. I sat down on the bed and then she turned the light off, and it was black. Completely black.

I don't like the dark. I can see shapes moving around. They're not here when it's light, so I don't know why they always have to come out and scare me when it's dark. I hate it. I start to cry, but it won't do any good because she won't come and get me.

I know she's not going to change her mind and come up here and say something like, 'Sorry Vincent. I'm sorry I put you in there for not doing anything bad at all. It was all my fault.' And then give me a big hug, take me downstairs again and give me a glass of milk and one of her homemade biscuits.

No, that won't happen. I'll be here for ages, on my own, in the dark, with the moving shapes.

I don't know how long it's been now, how long I've sat here in the dark, but I can hear footsteps on the bare wooden stairs. She slows down when she gets near to the top and she stops and sighs. I can imagine her standing there, with her hands on her hips, her apron still tied around her waist, scowling at the thought of having to let me come downstairs again. I only know a lot of time has passed because my tummy keeps rumbling. It feels so hollow I think it might cave in on me. I might have missed one *meal, but it could even be two. I hope she lets me go down and have some tea.*

I'm prepared now for what's coming next. The last time I was in here for ages she came up and threw the light on, and my eyes hurt so much, I couldn't bear it. This time I know what to do. I turn my face into my pillow, so that when the light comes on I won't be blinded again.

Light on. Door open. Arm grabbed. And I'm back downstairs, without a word.

No milk. No biscuit. Just that look in her eyes that I can't run away from.

We Walk by Faith Not by Sight

*S*ometimes things don't look so clear to me. Sometimes my eyes can't see everything they used to. Bright lights look a bit dim, and the shiny cars on the way to school don't seem quite so shiny anymore. And my head hurts. Boy, it hurts so much, sometimes.

'I can't see properly,' I say to Barbara one day. 'I think I'm going blind.' She tuts and complains but she makes an appointment and off we go to see the doctor.

'What a nuisance you are,' she sighs, dragging me along the street. 'It isn't as though I've got time on my hands to waste, you know.'

I look up at her, but her face is a bit of a blur, and I can't see if her eyes have that empty look behind them today. I think it's best to say nothing so I just keep quiet.

The pavements are wet and slippery so I'm glad she's holding onto me, but my hand is starting to hurt because she's gripping it so hard. 'You're such an inconvenience, you know. There are so *many better things I could be getting on with today. A burden, that's what you are. Nobody wants you. Even your own mother didn't want you, did she?'*

She goes on and on and I say nothing and keep walking. My head is so sore. It hurts to talk. Hurts to do anything.

It smells funny in the doctor's room. I work out that it's coming from his suit, because whenever I go near him it makes my eyes water, and then I can see even less. It's the same smell as the stuff Barbara puts in the cupboards in her house, to keep away the moths. It keeps away everything, even people, if you ask me. Disgusting smell, it is.

I back away from the doctor because of that smell, and I can tell he's cross about this.

'Come here, boy,' he grumbles. 'How am I supposed to look at your eyes if you won't come near me?' He grabs me by the wrist and pulls me closer but every time I back away from him. I don't want to do this! I can't bear that smell! My eyes are stinging so much.

'Nothing wrong with this boy,' the doctor says to Barbara. 'I suggest you box his ears and send him back to school right away.'

'Another fine waste of my time that was,' says Barbara, as she drags me back along the street towards the school. 'Nothing wrong with you, he says.' She makes strange tutting noises again, shaking her head all the time. 'Honestly, I really could do without this. You're a liar, boy, that's what you are. I don't want to hear any more of this, do you understand?'

I can't seem to do anything right now. Whatever I do, it's the wrong thing. Even if little Margaret does something bad, I get the blame for that too. So I just stay quiet and keep my head down. It's easier that way.

School is the best place to be, just because I'm out of the way and they don't tell me off all the time. I'm surprised they don't, though, because I don't do my work, like I'm supposed to. Because I can't see to do my work, so I don't do it. It hurts to do anything now. It hurts when I talk, it hurts when I go outside into the bright sunshine. Sometimes I feel like my head is going to explode. I sit at my desk with my head in my hands and I daydream. I can't even stare out of the window because it's too bright.

When I get home she starts on me again.

'Why haven't you done this? Why haven't you done that? Why, why, why?' That's what it feels like, all the time. School is my escape, although sometimes I wonder if one day a car might hit me on the way there, and then this would be all over. I can't see the cars, so I have to listen carefully for their noise and make sure I'm not in the way.

The only thing I do now is stay in my little room, all of the time. No smiling, no talking, no playing. All I want to do is stay away from the noise which makes my head hurt.

One day Barbara says to me: 'This isn't right, you know, all of this. I'm going to take you to see a specialist.' I don't know what a specialist is, but when we go back to the same room in that awful hospital where I went with my bad foot, I want to run away.

'Try to get yourself across the room,' a voice says to me. So I follow their voices, and I do manage to get to them.

'Well, he can do that alright,' says the doctor.

Then I have to play a game where I have to post things in and out of a box. They don't say if I've done it right or not. They don't say anything about that at all.

'We're going to send him away to a special school for problem boys,' the doctor says finally. 'They will know what to do with him, because we don't.'

I'm not a problem boy. I'm just a boy who can't see, and who nobody wants.

That evening I go up to my room and I shut the door. I always do a lot of thinking in here, because there's not much else I can do. I've learnt about God at school, and I would like to think that he is real, but if he is real, then why does he let a little child like me suffer?

Each night I say the same prayer, but I don't know if God is listening to me or not:

'Dear God,

If you exist, either send me back to the nuns or take me home, but please don't leave me here any longer, for I cannot bear it any more.'

I think my voice sounds like I'm begging instead of praying, but I don't care, because I'm so lonely. Anywhere would be better than here.

Wherever this special school is, I really want to go there. God must have heard my prayers after all.

Today I'm leaving. They're not sorry to see me go, I can tell. They're trying not to smile as we say goodbye, but there are smiles are in their eyes. They're glad to see the back of me at last.

Maybe I'm being sent away to die. Maybe that's why the school is special, because little boys like me go there to die. But I'm not afraid of that. Sometimes dying doesn't scare me as much as living does.

Living isn't such a great thing when everything hurts and nobody loves you.

In the Company of Angels

N uns had looked after me at the start of my life, and at the age of ten I was to go to St Joseph's School at Croome Court, where they would look after me again. At each new turn my life took, I was always hopeful that better times were ahead, and now I believed these nuns were to be my salvation.

My memories of arriving at Croome for the first time are rather sketchy. I was up early that morning, ready with my little suitcase all packed, and I can recall going on the Tube to Paddington Station, which was a new and exciting experience for me. But Barbara was cross, as she always seemed to be, because it interfered with her day and was inconvenient for her again. I had no idea what was happening and no one told me where we were going.

It must have been at Paddington Station that I first set eyes on Sister Ursula. Barbara had wandered off and left me standing on my own like a little statue, and I could just about make out this shady shape in front of me. She knelt down, took my hand and reassured me that I would be safe. It didn't take me long to realise that she was the loveliest and kindest lady I had ever met. I think she soon realised that I needed special help, and she took it upon herself to give me that help. I believed her to be an angel and thought that my prayers must have been answered.

We sat on the train together, Sister Ursula and I, looking out of the window, in as much as I could see anything. Most of it was blurry to me, just streaks of colour and flashes of light flying past. Pershore station seemed very small compared to Paddington, and a coach was waiting for us there to take us to the school. Sister Ursula held my hand the whole time.

I was exhausted by the time we arrived at the school, late in the afternoon. We were shepherded into a large room and made to strip down completely, which was very demeaning. Even after all the humiliation I had already suffered in my young life, I felt as though my own soul had been stripped from my body. We were then assigned a number, and this was often used through our time at the school, in place of our names. Looking back on it now, it's unimaginable – more like being a concentration camp inmate or a prisoner, than a schoolboy.

All of our own clothes and personal possessions – even our teddies – were put in our suitcases and taken away and we were then examined before being given a new set of school clothes. I say new, but actually they weren't new at all. The shorts were really scratchy, like sacking almost. I don't think there really was a proper uniform as such – the shirts and jumpers were ones that people had donated – although everyone had those same awful, itchy shorts. I was too poorly to complain, and as I needed help with changing, Sister Ursula helped me and we just got on with it.

I had always been terrified of adults, but for some reason I didn't think of nuns as being human, so I wasn't frightened of them. And particularly not of Sister Ursula, who was so kind. I hadn't spoken the whole way there, and clung to her now as though my life depended on it. I knew that if I stayed close to her then I would be alright. I remember, too, the kindness of the other children, which was something I wasn't used to at all.

No one told me why I had been sent there, but I was used to being herded around without any explanation and I accepted it for what it was. For a young child whose sight was very poor, it was even more traumatic. It ought to have been exciting for me, being surrounded by boys of my own age for the first time in my life, but instead I found the noise and buzz of the other children frightening. I half expected that at some point, someone would come and beat me for doing something wrong, even though I had no idea what was expected of me. It confused me even further when the anticipated beating did not happen.

Once we had changed into our uniforms, a boy called Ian was asked to show me to the playing field. He took me by the hand and led me through to a stable yard, and then as any young child would do, he let go of my hand and ran off to play with his friends. No one could blame him for that, but I was frozen to the spot, with no idea where I was or what I should do.

The sun's glare hurt my eyes so much. I covered them with one hand and stumbled to the wall, feeling my way gingerly along it with my other hand. When I ran out of wall to hang onto, I fell over. I picked myself up and groped my way back to the wall.

One of the nuns, Sister Paul, was sitting on a log supervising some of the boys. She saw what happened and sent one of them over to fetch me. The boy took my hand and led me to her, and I remember her putting her arm around me and how safe it made me feel.

By now I was very conscious of being quite different to the other children. I knew there was something wrong with me and for the first time in my life I could sense that people were beginning to notice this, too. Although that was a positive step, I now felt as though my weaknesses were exposed for all to see. I was particularly aware of this when various boys and nuns led me around the school by my hand, as I was unable to go anywhere on my own. God bless those boys, they seemed to know that I needed their help and they never hesitated to go out of their way to give it.

Sister Ursula took a particular interest in me right from the start, and during the first couple of days she summoned me to do a little test, which she called the Game of Distance.

'Stand still, Vincent,' she said. 'And tell me when you can't see me anymore.' And so saying, she began to back away from me. I think she only managed four feet or so before I could barely see her. By then she had become the shadow of a person, but I didn't tell her this, because I still hadn't spoken since I'd arrived at the school. So I simply nodded.

She took me into the classroom and sat me at the front of the class, very close to her desk. I don't think she expected me to do very much, and I couldn't have done if I'd wanted to – I couldn't see well enough to do any schoolwork at all.

At lunchtime Sister Ursula took me to see the school nurse. She asked the nurse to check my medical records and find out when I last had an eye test.

'Never,' came the nurse's reply. I remember that there wasn't much of a folder on me at all. I imagine it only contained the addresses of the places I had stayed thus far in my little life; no one had ever taken enough interest in me to write up a fat dossier and I had never stayed in one place for long enough for it to be an issue. The sum total of my life to date amounted to just a few sheets of paperwork.

For You Have Been Born Again

Today they are taking me in an ambulance to the hospital. Sister Ursula is by my side and there is no way I would go there without her. She's so kind, but sometimes I don't understand why. What have I done to deserve her being so nice to me?

At the hospital they hand me something which looks like a dress. 'What's this?' I say to Sister Ursula.

She looks really surprised, because these are the first words I've spoken to her — to anyone — since I arrived at the school.

'Oh my goodness, you can speak!' she says, and she claps her hands together. I like it that she is pleased.

'I can speak,' I say, 'but it hurts my head, so I don't.'

'Well, this is a hospital gown, and if you put it on then we can go and see the nice doctor.'

In the doctor's room, Sister Ursula asks me to play the same Game of Distance that we had played before.

'Now could you read the letters on the wall, please Vincent?' says the doctor afterwards.

'What letters?' I say.

After that first trip to the hospital we spend many months going back and forward to see the doctor. I can't see very well, obviously, but I have a special way of working out where I am in the hospital. In the waiting room there are rows of chairs bolted to the floor and I know that if I walk down to the yellow chair, sit in the front row and turn sideways, put my hand out and take three steps forward, then I will get to the doctor. It makes me feel safe and I do this every time I go there.

'Here he goes, he's off again,' the nurses say, smiling at me as I do my chair trick. I know where I am and where I'm going, so I'm fine.

Today is a special day because we are going to the hospital again, but this time I have to stay there, because they want to do an operation on my head. I don't really understand what that means, but if it will make me better, then I will let them do it, because I really want to get better now.

They lead me into a big room – a ward, they call it – where there are six beds. Between the beds are panels with Mickey Mouse and Tom and Jerry on them. I'm a bit big for pictures like that, really, but I don't say anything, because I know they're trying to make it nice for us.

'Hello, Vincent,' says a nurse. 'I'm just going to do a few little tests, to make sure you are ready for the operation.'

I can hear some of the other children giggling behind the nurse's back.

'Why are they laughing at you?' I say.

'Because I'm black,' she says. I don't know what to say to this, and nor do I understand why the colour of someone's skin means you should laugh at them, or why it makes her any different to the rest of us. She's kind, and that's all I care about. I can't see properly what colour her skin is, but whatever it is, it doesn't matter to me, not one bit.

'I like you,' I say to this nurse. 'You're nice to me.'

I can hear the smile in the nurse's voice and from that moment on I know she is going to be on my side and I'm very glad of that.

A few hours later a new girl comes onto the ward, and they put her in the bed the other side of the panel from mine. She's a little bit on her own there, because she can't see any of the other children, and when her parents leave she starts to cry.

I want to go and help her and so I use her crying as a beacon to guide me around the panel to the side of her bed.

'Why are you crying?' I say.

'Because I've never been on my own and I'm really scared,' she says. I take her by the hand and somehow we manage to go and find the nurse. I'm looking after her, and she is guiding me. We're a team and together we make it.

'Please could we swap beds?' I say to the nurse. 'I'm used to being on my own and I don't mind if she wants to go in my bed, where she can see all the other children.'

'Of course you can,' says the nurse. 'How kind you are, Vincent.'

I don't mind the other bed. I'm not locked in a room and I can hear the children's voices around me, so it's a kind of freedom for me, still.

They do a lot of tests on me over the next few days and then one day, a very frightening thing happens. They take me from my bed and into a room, and without any warning they put a bib around my head and shave off all my hair. They don't tell me why, and so the next day when they take me into a room they call the operating theatre, I'm really worried that something bad is going to happen to me.

The doctor starts to fix a lot of tubes and wires to me, and then they wedge me into a seat with some special cushions.

'It's really important that you don't move,' says the doctor. 'Now, we will put some special chemicals on your head, and you need to tell us when you can't feel anything.'

After about five minutes my head is so numb that I can't feel a thing when they touch it.

'We're keeping you awake while we do this operation,' says the surgeon. 'We need to do that because we need the light from your eyes to help us do our job. We can't turn the lights in the room up too brightly, or they will hurt your eyes.'

It kind of makes sense to me, but I'm very frightened. He puts a disc around my head – I feel like an angel wearing a halo – and a green cloth, which hangs over my eyes a little bit. I try to brush it away, but one of the doctors tells me not to.

A nurse sits down beside me.

'Now, Vincent,' she says. We're going to start the operation. It's really, really important that you don't move. You do understand that, don't you?'

'Yes,' I say. I can't nod or shake my head now so I have to speak.

I know that the surgeon is cutting into my head, but I can't feel any pain, just a strange kind of pressure from the drill, pushing down hard on my skull. All the time my lovely, kindly nurse speaks to me, telling me that everything will be alright, and making sure that I don't move at all.

There are some young people watching me. My nurse had said there would be medical students in the room, because they can learn a lot from watching an operation like mine. I know all about the students because I've seen them before. The White Coat Gang, I call them. They go around the hospital with the older doctors and learn all about the illnesses that the patients have. It's how they learn to be good doctors themselves.

Now I can hear them discussing me, though, and I don't like it very much. I don't have any choice, I can't tell them to go away, but I wish they would stop talking about me like I'm not in the room.

'When we go ahead with the operation,' I hear the surgeon say to them, 'it might of course blind him. Or another outcome could be that it's just too late for him. If that's the case, then we will just have to close up and wait for the inevitable to happen.'

I don't really know what the inevitable is, but I do understand that they're saying I might die, or if I don't, then I might not be able to see. Either way, it doesn't sound very nice.

'Or there might be some brain damage,' the surgeon says now. 'In which case this child will be institutionalised for what remains of his life. Or worst case, he could simply die on the operating table. Maximum chance of survival is around twenty percent.'

I understand enough of that to know it's not good, but there's no going back now. They're drilling into my head and I have to let them.

The operation seems to go on for a while and now I'm feeling really tired. The surgeon does a strange thing – he seems to be able to control my arms and legs without me doing anything at all. I'm like one of those puppets with strings all over the place, only I haven't got strings, just a surgeon who can see my brain and who can touch different parts of it to make me do things. It's a really odd feeling.

A while later I wake up. I remember how it suddenly went dark before, like no darkness I've ever known, and I thought it was death coming for me. But now I'm awake, so I know I have cheated death this time.

My head hurts so much. So very, very much, more than ever before. It has a big bandage round it which I can feel when I clutch the sides of my head in pain.

'I'm going to be sick,' I say. The little girl I helped before is sitting beside my bed with a sick bowl in her lap and she passes it to me. She is like a tiny little nurse, and every time I'm sick she is there for me, helping me through it and holding my hand afterwards.

45

They say I have to spend a long time in bed now and that it might take me a while to get better, but that's fine, because I haven't got the energy to do anything, anyway.

'He was very lucky,' I hear them say. None of this feels lucky to me, but I know that what they mean is that I might have died in there.

Every day the little girl sits with me. I don't know what she's in here for, and she did tell me her name, but I keep forgetting it because my head hurts so much. It doesn't matter, anyway, because she's my kind little friend and I really like her.

Soon I'm feeling well enough to talk to her, and we chat a while some days. It's nice to have a friend.

Then one day I wake up and I don't have a headache anymore. It's amazing! I've been with that pain for so long, it has almost become a part of me, and so to wake up without it is weird.

Today I have some visitors. Three nuns have arrived to see me – Sister Ursula, Sister Paul and the Mother Superior.

'I've brought you a present, Vincent,' says Sister Ursula.

I unwrap the parcel and inside is a toy Mini, with a chessboard roof and doors. It's the best present I've ever had and I love it. I get straight out of my bed to play with it on the floor.

'Well, I can see someone's feeling a little better,' says Sister Ursula, and she has a big smile on her face. 'It's nearly time to go home, Vincent.' I know that home means back to the school, but that's fine. Sister Ursula will be there, so I'm happy about that. I will be sad to say goodbye to my little friend, but glad to get back to the boys at the school.

The trouble is, I don't want them to see me with no hair. I hated having my hair shaved off, and I don't like it that my head is bald now. There are seven of us like this, all with no hair, because we all had the same operation.

'Please don't let them see me looking like this,' I say to the doctors one day. 'They will all laugh at me.' When you've lived all over the place, you just want to look like everyone else, and not look different.

'No one will laugh at you, Vincent,' says one of the doctors. 'And anyway, I have a great idea.'

The next day the doctor comes in and he has Coventry caps for us all to wear, to cover our bare heads. We think it's great when we all put our caps on and we look the same.

'Now you will be alright, won't you?' says the doctor. 'You're the Cappie gang, you see. No one will know that you haven't got any hair, and pretty soon it will all grow back.'

I'm quite excited about going back to school now, and when I get there I tell my friends that I'm part of the Cappie gang and they think that's cool.

I soon settle back into school and my hair starts to grow again. My favourite place to go – my safe place – is under the big tree in the front field. Now that the sun doesn't hurt my eyes anymore, it's good to be outside, and I love it. I talk to people more now, and it doesn't hurt my head when I do.

Every day I try to go a little further. I head off, away from the tree, and see how far I can get before I have to turn around again.

Over the other side from the football pitch is the meadow, and once I can get that far on my own, I spend ages looking at the little flowers. They are just so tiny and perfect.

'You're doing all the things now that a small child would do,' says Sister Ursula. 'You're marvelling at things, because you haven't been able to see them properly before.'

Sometimes I spend hours there, and I'm always the last one to come in when the nuns call me.

One day I'm dawdling in the field as usual. The nuns don't mind this, they're kind to me about it, because they know how much I love looking at things, seeing all God's creations for the first time in my life.

Suddenly there's a deafening noise behind me and I jump out of my skin with fright. My heart beats fast and I put my hands over my ears and turn round slowly to see what horrors await me.

I let out a huge sigh when I see that it's just a load of birds, all swooping around together. I watch as they swirl about over my head. I'm not scared, now that I know what they are. Sister Ursula comes over and tells me that they are starlings, and they make a lot of noise when they flock together. Well I know that!

As we walk back to the school together I say to her:

'I've changed my mind and I want to stay.'

What I mean is that I want another chance at life, now that I feel so much better. I used to think that dying would be a way to escape from the pain, and that I had been sent here to die, but without the pain my life seems worth living again. I just needed a little time to think about that and now I know that it's true.

'I'm going to live and I'm going to get better,' I say to the Sister.

'Of course you are, Vincent,' she says. She really is a gift from God. Every day I count my blessings that they sent me here.

The Voice of an Angel

I *couldn't speak much before the operation. It was just too painful. My jaw hurt and my head hurt and so I got used to keeping quiet. It was easier that way.*

Now that I've had the operation it's much easier. I find it easier to speak and I want to speak, and I'm really enjoying that, but at times I really struggle to get the words out. I try so hard, but sometimes the word sticks and the same sound keeps coming, like I'm saying tr..tr..tree, instead of just tree. Sister Ursula tells me that it's called a stutter. Even that word itself a really hard word to say, because I can't get the first sound of that out either. I never used to stutter, back in the old days before the operation. Back when I used to speak, before the pain got too bad.

So she says to me one day: 'Vincent, I'd really like you to join my choir.'

I'm not really sure what happens in a choir, but I decide that if Sister Ursula wants me to do it, then it must be a good thing, because she's always so nice and never suggests anything bad. And you never know, it might just be fun.

There are about ten of us in the choir, and we sing some nice songs, really we do. Some of the songs are a little bit boring and churchy, but others are a bit more cheerful, and they're the ones I like best. The happy songs.

'La la la,' I go, singing along with the tunes, until I've learnt the words properly. It's really fun. At the end of the songs I like to make the other boys laugh by adding in a couple of really high notes. Sister Ursula doesn't tell me off, she just smiles. I think she's glad that I'm having fun.

'Have you noticed what's happening when you sing, Vincent?' she asks me one day.

I think she's going to say something about me being a bit of a pickle with those high notes, but it's not that at all.

'Well, when you sing, you don't stutter, do you?'

'No, I suppose I don't,' I say.

'I think it's because you're concentrating so hard on the words and the music that you forget to stutter. I'm so pleased about that, Vincent. Isn't it wonderful?'

I have to say I haven't really noticed, but now that she mentions it I do, and I give her a big smile.

'You also have a lovely singing voice, young man,' she says now, and I glow with pride. 'I'd like you to come and learn a new song every week, and we will soon get rid of that stutter once and for all.'

And so Sister Ursula teaches me songs, and these things which she calls scales, which go up and down and have a lot of notes in them, and how to breathe properly when I'm singing. It makes me really happy, learning it all.

One day she comes and tells me that I have to do a very special thing. I'm to go and sing in St Chad's Cathedral, in front of the Archbishop of Birmingham, at the Christmas festival. It all sounds so grand and wonderful that I can't quite believe it to start with, and I think she can tell that from the look on my face.

'Yes, it's true,' she says. 'You are going to sing at the festival, Vincent, and won't that be a marvellous thing to do?'

'But I don't really understand the words,' I say. 'And what is this thing called a cathedral?'

Sister Ursula tells me that the song is in a language called Latin, and that I don't have to understand it, I just need to learn all the words and sing them as best I possibly can. And a cathedral is like a church, only huge, she says, but she says it like huuuuuuuge, and she rolls her eyes up to the ceiling.

Then the day of the festival comes and I go in the car with Sister Ursula and Mother Superior and we go to Birmingham.

'Wow, this place is huuuuuge,' I say, in the same way that Sister Ursula said it. I never knew such enormous buildings could exist! I have to put on a special outfit, and there are lots of other children there dressed like me, with a frilly collar and a special white robe and a big medallion around my neck. I feel like an angel, I really do!

'I'll sit in the front row,' says Sister Ursula, 'so that I'm really close to you. There's no need to be nervous. When it's time to sing, look at me and pretend that the rest of this place is empty.'

52

So I do that, and it works! I sing my little heart out and I love it so much.

When we get back to the school Sister Ursula tells everyone how good I was and I'm puffed up with pride.

'You sang Ave Maria so beautifully today,' she tells me before I go up to bed. 'And your stutter went away, didn't it? You can overcome this, Vincent, I know you can. If you can sing in Birmingham cathedral in front of all those people, then you can overcome anything.'

Now I have another very special thing to go to. I've been chosen to go to the London Palladium where a lady called Cleo Laine is performing. Sister Ursula tells me she's very famous, and also that she does a lot of good things for children in the care system. I like the idea of that.

So we go to the Palladium and it's also very huge, though not as big as the cathedral in Birmingham. There are lots of other children there, and we have to dance in the background while the Cleo lady sings a song called 'Children of the World.'

I like being the chosen one instead of the forgotten one.

Solo Angel

In 2012, at one of the school reunions, a fellow former pupil asked me to try to explain the differences between an ordinary child and a child who has been through the care system. I thought for a moment, and then decided that I would write something down and send it to him. I needed time to get it right, because he wanted to use my description to explain to other people what effect the care system had on children. The previous evening I had watched a film about Yellowstone National Park through the seasons, and on the train on the way home from the reunion it seemed the obvious thing to use that park as the analogy for my story.

This is what I wrote down that day:

A child with a family is carried by his mother and father for his first year, and eventually learns to stand on his own two feet.

Imagine that his journey is five hundred miles long, and to give an example, I would compare it to a journey through the Yellowstone National Park. The child's father is his guardian and his mother is his guide, and the parents know that, for their child, the journey will be relatively safe, because they know the pitfalls and the safe ways to cross the park. The weather conditions might change, but they are prepared for it. If they follow the North Star, then they will get there eventually.

The child is carrying a metaphorical stick on his journey, and his goal is to one day be as tall as that stick. Once he gets to the same height as the stick then he is an adult and his journey through childhood – and through the park – has come to an end.

For a child in care, the only thing he knows is that he must follow the North Star. His journey to adulthood begins whilst he is still very small, compared to his stick. He doesn't have the luxury of his own guardian and guide. Even in his first year he is passed from person to person, until he can walk on his own.

His instinct tells him to follow the North Star, but he is a solo angel and must walk alone. He has no idea what time he should start his journey, so he starts it later than most. He has no idea where the shelters are, nor the pitfalls sent to trip him up, nor the shortcuts which will get him onto the easier path. He can always hear the pack of wolves baying in the background.

The boy is in summer clothing but didn't realise that he should also have taken his winter clothing along. Innocently he presumes that every day the sun will shine.

After a while the boy meets up with other children like himself. They huddle together in groups and continue their journey as a pack. They don't know what lies ahead, but they do know that they must keep going. They don't realise the weather is changing and they can still hear the wolves howling.

The seasons change and the weather turns, storms come, and still the children keep going, together but all alone. The storm forces them to drift apart occasionally, and sometimes they hear a scream in the distance, but they cannot afford to stop.

And then the storm abates and the children can stand upright again. At that point they realise they are as tall as their sticks. When they look around to see who is still with them, some of their friends are missing.

Now for the first time they starting talking to one another, and they make a pledge that when they have their own children, they will never abandon them. Their children will never be allowed to hear the wolves baying, and not know the way of safety on their journey.

This is the only way I can explain how the care system felt for me.

Tears Of God

*I*t's a nice sunny day. It's May, and the trees have lots of pretty blossom on them, but although it's lovely outside, I'm sad on the inside.

I've come into the church and I'm sitting underneath the altar. It's my quiet place to hide, when I want to get away from everyone and everything. I like to come in here and think, and it makes me calm again if something upsets me.

And today something has upset me. They just told me I won't be going back, and I'm really sad about that. I won't be going back to Norfolk, not ever, and it makes me feel all wobbly inside because that's the only place I've ever really known, apart from here at the school. I had a really nice holiday placement with a policemen and his wife in Norfolk, and it did feel to me like the place I'd come from. But they've told me I can't go back to them either, but I don't know why.

I know I can't stay here at the school forever, too. One day I'll be too old and then even Sister Ursula won't be able to make them let me stay.

I can't stay here and Norfolk won't have me. I'm miles from the place that I thought was my home. I look up at the cross and I ask God: 'Why, if all children are gifts, does no one want me?'

Then the door creaks open and a nun comes in. It's Sister Elizabeth, and I'm quite pleased about that, because she's one of the nice ones. She looks a bit sad to see me sitting alone, and she comes and sits down next to me, on the altar steps. She doesn't say anything to begin with, because she knows that the best way with me is to just be quiet and let me speak in my own time. 'Patience,' they all say, when they're trying to work out what to do with me.

'If children are gifts from God, what's wrong with me?' This time I ask Sister Elizabeth, not God.

She says: 'There are some people in this world who don't understand that when they are given a gift, it is from God. God sheds a tear for the children who are turned away, and that's why you are here with us.'

'OK, then,' I say. 'It's time to move on and forget.' I get up and I go out of the church. I know that when I'm big, when I'm a grown-up man, I will feel the same way about moving on and forgetting about things.

Bless All the Dear Children

I'm twelve now. It's nearly Christmas. I don't have anywhere to go for the holidays, and lots of the boys have gone home already. It's getting quite quiet at St Joseph's. A bit lonely. Three coaches came and most of the children went on them, including my best friend, so I haven't been up to much. I sit and look out of the window a lot, wishing there was someone to run about with.

'We've found you somewhere, Vincent,' says Sister Ursula one day. She folds her hands quietly in front of her.

'Why can't I stay here with you?' I ask. I don't really understand when she tells me I can't, because I thought all the nuns stayed here over the holidays. Maybe they don't. Maybe they have to go and do their nun stuff somewhere else, and that's why the children have to go away.

'It's a nice place to go, Vincent,' says Sister Ursula. 'It's in Kent.'

I don't know what 'In Kent' means.

'Will there be other children there?' I say. It will be alright if there are, I suppose.

I pack my little case and they take me to this place called Kent. It's quite a long way away. A man takes me. He's a young priest, they tell me, on his way to go and work there, in Kent, so he's the one who drives me there.

I get out of the car and I stand and look at the house. I'm feeling a bit nervous now. I really hope they're nice. It's quite a big house. Someone tells me later that it's two houses which have been knocked through, so that there is more space for the children who live there. Then the door opens and lots of faces peer out to look at me. I count six children, two girls and four boys. One of the boys comes forward. He looks about my age.

'Have you come to stay for Christmas?' he asks. He doesn't wait for me to reply but he seems quite excited about my arrival. Maybe it won't be so bad here after all, and it's only for a couple of weeks. Then I can go back to Sister Ursula.

This boy tells me the other children's names. One of the boys is his brother and the two of them tell me that they have lived there all their lives.

'What, don't you go away to school?' I ask. 'I have to sleep at my school. I'm only here because it's Christmas and I can't stay at the school over Christmas.'

'We live here all the time, and we go to school nearby,' says the boy.

It's Christmas morning. I'm not expecting any presents. I don't normally get anything, so I don't see why this year will be any different. I tiptoe down the stairs, rubbing the sleep from my eyes, and I can hear that the other children are already down in the lounge. There's a lot of laughter, and a crackly sound, like paper makes when you screw it up.

I don't want to get in the way and spoil their fun, so I go into the kitchen. I lean against the worktop and look out into the little garden. It's quite nice here, really, but there's not as much space to run around as there is at school. There's a bird swinging on a long tube of nuts, and I think how lucky that little bird is, to be so free. As long as he has food and he can fly around, then he's happy.

Then the lady comes into the kitchen.

'Good morning, Vincent, and a very Merry Christmas to you!' she says cheerily. She pats me on the shoulder and I look up at her jolly face. She's a nice lady, really kind.

'Merry Christmas,' I say, unsure what I should do next.

Then she pulls something out from behind her back. 'This is for you,' she says, handing me a present.

'For me?' I say. I am so surprised, I don't really know what to do or say. My breath seems to have left my body, and there's a funny prickly feeling around my eyes.

'Yes, for you. Open it, then!' she says.

I'm a bit slow at first, and then I rip off the paper, throwing it to the floor.

I look at the present in wonder. It's a Rolf Harris record. No one has ever bought me much before, and I've certainly never had my own record.

There's a record player here, and I play my new album every day. It makes me so happy, to think that someone gave this to me. Just to me! How kind they are here.

But the day I have to leave comes round all too soon.

I know I can't take my present with me, because personal possessions aren't allowed at school, just your clothes and your shoes.

'What shall I do with this?' I ask the lady, as I'm about to leave. 'What do you do with the things that get left behind?'

'Well, you know about the box under the stairs, Vincent,' she says. She gives me a little hug, because she can see I don't want to leave my present behind.

'You mean the box for the unexpected?' I say.

'Yes,' she replies. 'I always keep a box of things for the children who arrive on Christmas Eve. If you put your present in there, then it will be a gift for a child who comes unexpectedly next Christmas Eve.'

I know that already, because this year I am the unexpected child.

Someone comes to take me back to school, but I really hope I can come back here again one day.

I Will Not Be Afraid

My time at St Joseph's was on the whole happy and transformative, but sadly that was not the case for everyone. I know that a lot has come to light recently about abuse at St Joseph's, and it's up to those involved to tell their story, not me. My purpose in this book isn't to add fuel to that particular fire, but merely to tell my own story, however there are some episodes which come to mind that I still feel I need to mention.

Sometimes the levels of chastisement got out of control. Most of the younger nuns were very nice – Sister Ursula included – however many of the older ones were more set in their ways about how the boys should be disciplined. They could be very cynical and quite aggressive and if a boy was strong-willed then he would stand out as a target.

Bearing in mind that I could only see a few feet in front of me when I first arrived at Croome, I could sometimes hear children crying as Mother Superior disciplined them. I'm not sure what she did to these boys, but clearly it was painful.

My friend Michael was quite hard of hearing and one of the nuns would take great delight in walking up behind him and hitting him hard on the head, before carrying on walking. There seemed to be no reason for it; it was just something she enjoyed doing. Michael became a very nervous boy, as you can imagine.

One night there was a new boy in the dormitory and Sister Paulinus was on duty. This boy didn't know that you must never say no to a nun, and I didn't hear what she asked him, but the next thing I knew she had pushed me hard to one side, grabbed the bed and tipped it over. Many of the boys escaped out of the dormitory but I remember this new boy coming back later with a lot of bruises and our beds had all been turned upside down.

We knew that this wasn't right, but we just got on with things and didn't make a fuss, as you did in those days. We survived, and we had good moments as well as the bad. I remember one boy saying, 'Whatever they do, they can't destroy us, because it's our turn to live.'

I'm sorry now for those who are scarred by what happened to them, and it does make me struggle to reconcile this kind of treatment with religion.

When we arrived back at school after the holidays, we were always really wired, and we would sit in circles on the back field and talk about what had happened to us while we were away.

Sometimes we would have novice nuns arrive at the school. We could tell they were new, because they were always dressed in light blue. They tended not to stay very long, presumably just passing through as part of their training.

I must have been about twelve one time when we were sitting in our group, chatting about our holidays. I have to say that the things we discussed wouldn't be what most kids of that age would talk about.

One of these young nuns came to sit in our group as we talked about our experiences, which included sexual abuse, violence, and how one boy's hair had been set on fire. It wasn't just one child's who had been through such awful things, but many of us had suffered. We had almost forgotten that the nun was there, because to us, this kind of discussion wasn't abnormal. But then we saw her reaction to it. She turned white and scurried away. She didn't stay for long at the school.

What dreadful things we all went through, but to us it was just a part of life.

The Vincent Tree

When I first arrived at St Joseph's it was obvious to everyone that I wouldn't be capable of doing any kind of sport. During my first few days the boys took it upon themselves to be my guides, but naturally, at playtime, they wanted to run and burn off their own energy. No one could blame them for that.

So the boys reached a simple conclusion on how to deal with this dilemma. At the front of the house there is a tree. The boys had already noticed that the sunlight aggravated my eyes, so they decided that the best way to look out for me and still have fun of their own was to deposit me under the tree, in the shade, and tell me to stay there until it was time to go back. At that point they would come and fetch me.

That suited me down to the ground! It meant that I could feel safe amongst the boys and be out of the sunshine. The nuns noticed that I would stay there while the boys went to play and that some of the younger boys would sometimes sit with me and keep me company. In the end, they would always wander off to play, though.

At one point I had to be in the hospital wing of the school, and one boy, George, would carry me down and sit me under the tree. Sister Ursula would also sit there with me whenever the boys had P.E. I came to think of it as my tree, and I loved spending time there with Sister Ursula. I didn't realise at the time, but she would use those moments to assess how I was doing, and make a decision about what to do with me. I was very defensive at first and didn't give much away, but soon I began to open up to her, and I looked forward to the days when the boys were doing sports, so that we could have our chats.

I remember one occasion in particular. It was in late spring, and I'd had my operation by that time, but I still wasn't fit enough to join in with the other boys. My recuperation was very slow. And then I developed the stutter, which sometimes put me off talking to her. Anyone who spoke to me had to be very patient.

I told Sister Ursula about the kind nurse in the hospital, and how mean the other children had been to her because of the colour of her skin. To this day I will never forget what she said to me:

'Vincent, in your life to come you will meet many people of many colours. They will look different to you, they might even dress differently to you, or speak different languages, eat different food, and come from different cultures and backgrounds.

'I've learnt one very simple thing, Vincent,' she continued, looking me directly in the eye. 'Now this is important, and I want you to listen very carefully and take heed of what I say.

'When you meet someone you've never seen before, regardless of what they look like, give them a little bit of respect. You don't know who you're talking to, and if they don't deserve your respect, then that will soon be revealed to you. And it's at that point, and only at that point, that you should brush the dust off your feet and walk away. There are millions of people out there who would like to talk to you and be your friend, so I'm pleased you did not feel any hatred. All you saw was a kind lady trying to look after you and doing her best to make you feel safe.

'I now understand,' she said, 'why, when we came to visit you, this nurse was so full of praise for you. When we first spoke to her she called you her little White Angel. Well, Vincent, we had been looking for a nickname for you, and I think this is most appropriate!'

I was so pleased to hear this, and I knew that Sister Ursula was proud of me for behaving like I did in the hospital, even though I was so desperately ill.

I have passed this story down to my own children and I pray that they pass it on to theirs. There is a very simple moral to the story, in that you should always judge a man by what he does, not by his skin colour, what he wears or how he speaks.

I have kept to that code all my life. I've met many people, good and bad, and those conversations with Sister Ursula, under that tree, are always uppermost in my mind.

It's probably the kind of thing a parent should teach their child. But I had no parents, just Sister Ursula. I am so lucky to have had her in my life.

In 2011, I went to the first reunion of former pupils of St Joseph's, at Croome Court. One of the men, called Les, caught up with me and pointed to the tree.

'There's the Vincent tree,' he said.

That tree had left its mark on us all.

Boys Will Be Boys

Once I was back to full health, I was a normal young boy again, and up to mischief like any other child. There are many stories I could tell of the antics we got up to, but here are just a few that stand out:

Jamjam and the Statues
At the back of the school there was an orchard, beautifully planted out, but the children weren't allowed to go in there, it was just for the nuns, for quiet contemplation. There were little religious statues under the trees, and the nuns would kneel down and pray in front of them. Myself and my mate, Jamjam, decided one day that we would play a trick on the nuns. We wondered what would happen if we moved the statues around. Commando mission time, we called it.

Jamjam was on guard duty and I slipped in, moved the statues around and sneaked out again.

For a whole week nothing was said, and it was a bit nerve-wracking. Then two weeks had passed and still nothing had been said, and we were even more scared. We thought the Mother Superior must be waiting for the right moment, and she certainly was. The following Monday morning she stormed into assembly, stood on the little stage, and screamed at the top of her voice, 'Who moved my statues!' We could practically see the steam coming out of her ears. Jamjam and I tried to shrink down behind all the other boys and make ourselves invisible.

We expected to get our comeuppance there and then, but nobody spoke up against us, and so we got away with it! We really felt we had scored a point against the nuns that day.

Jamjam got his nickname because he was of Asian origin and none of us could pronounce his name. However whenever there was jam for tea, he was there like a shot, and if you didn't get there quickly, he would eat the lot. Sadly I haven't been able to track him down in recent years, because I don't know his real name.

The M5 and the Great Escape
During one particularly awful school holiday I was sent to the Nazareth Centre in Nottingham. Here there was cruelty at every turn, and when I defended a child who

was being attacked, his adult attacker told me that if I ever came back there again, I wouldn't be leaving.

Anyway, once I'd been back at Croome for a couple of weeks we were allowed to go and watch the grand opening of the M5. Even though this brand new motorway was being build right through the centre of the Croome Estate, none of us knew anything about it, so it was very exciting. Around the same time, I was learning how to ride a bicycle.

'Motorway,' I said to my friend, Billy, one day. 'Hmmm.'

'Bicycles,' he said to me in return. 'Hmmm.'

'Not much on that motorway,' I said. 'Interesting.' The same naughty thought had popped into both our heads at the same time.

Then it dawned on me that if I was ever sent back to the Nazareth Centre, I wasn't going to make it out of there alive, and that was incentive enough for us to plan our escape.

So myself, Billy and his brother Jimmy, plus one other boy, stole the bicycles from the shed one evening. And off we peddled, up the M5. No cars, just us four scallywags on our bikes. Then suddenly there was a little blue and white police car behind us. We called those Jamjams too, in those days. Clearly we weren't terribly imaginative with our nicknames!

We didn't know until later, but there was a local newspaper reporter on the bridge, and he took photos of us. Billy's mother cut out the article and kept it, but sadly he can't now find it. How funny we must all have looked!

Obviously we didn't manage to escape, and we were taken back to Croome with our tails between our legs, expecting all hell to break loose from Mother Superior.

'My office, now!' she yelled.

We were all terrified, but what awaited us wasn't what we expected.

'Now boys, you all have nowhere to go, so why run away unless there's a reason?' she said.

So I told her all about my experiences at the Nazareth Centre, blurted it all out in one go.

'Sit down, Vincent, and tell me slowly,' she said. So I did.

'Well, if you promise never to play up again, then I will make sure you never go back there,' she said.

I kept to my word, and so did she.

The Swinging Sixties

One holiday, myself, Thomas and Jamjam were informed that we were off to London by train, and then on to Surrey. It was going to be a special treat for us all and we would be staying on a farm.

The farm looked like paradise when we arrived, and the lady who greeted us was lovely.

'Has the social worker gone yet?' she asked us.

'Yes,' we said.

'Well then, what on earth are you wearing? Come on, I'll sort you all out.'

I was given a pair of white trousers with red circles on them, and the other boys were given equally odd clothes.

'Weird,' I whispered to Jamjam. It wasn't the usual attire for a twelve year old boy.

'Come with me,' the lady said to us once we were all changed, and we walked over a big hill to the other side of the farm, where there were loads of tents.

'We're going to the circus!' we all thought.

It was early evening and everyone was dressed up in colourful clothes. Apart from the ones who were wearing nothing at all.

'She's got boobs!' said Thomas. 'Look!'

'So that's what they look like,' said Jamjam. Our eyes were on stalks, unable to take it all in.

We tucked into some more of the delicious mushrooms they'd given us and we laughed until our sides nearly split.

'This is brilliant,' I said, lying back on the grass. 'I wish we could stay forever.'

We must have fallen asleep at some point and the next day two big black police cars – Black Marias – came screeching down the driveway.

'Uh-oh, what's happened? What have we done?' we wondered. Being children in care, we always thought we were to blame.

I remember the social worker going apoplectic with rage. A policeman threw us into the back of the car and they drove us all the way back to school.

Our arrival back at Croome caused something of a stir. There we were, dressed like flower people, with painted platform shoes (we'd got hold of some aerosol cans in the night and gone wild with them), white sheepskin vests, and my glorious white trousers with the big red circles. We'd coloured our hair somehow, and our eyes were ringed with eyeliner.

'You've been with the devil,' yelled Mother Superior. 'You've been with the devil, so you have. Go and get yourselves cleaned up.'

'Whatever you say, Mother Superior,' we replied. I think at that stage we were still suffering from the after-effects of the drugs.

That night had to be the highlight of our little lives so far, getting to dress like hippies and watch naked women dancing around a fire in the middle of the night. Nothing else could compare!

Beyond St Joseph's

After Croome, I moved on to the senior school at Besford Court. This was a huge step for me in more ways than one. Medically I was fitter than I had been in my entire life, and there was something I needed to do to prove to myself just how well I was. During our first term at the senior school we were allowed to return occasionally to the junior school at Croome, to visit our friends. It was two and a half miles away and one day I decided that I was going to walk all the way back on my own. If I could do this, then I would know that I had finally turned a corner and was on my way back to normality. I did succeed, and from that moment onwards I never looked back. Those were my final steps towards recovery.

I left school, and the care of Social Services, on the last day of March 1971, the day before I turned sixteen.

I should have left sooner, but when the headmaster of Besford Court made contact with Norwich council's children's services, it seemed that my file hadn't been updated for many years. When they discovered that the family I had stayed with in my early years had split up and moved away, they knew that there was, quite literally, nowhere for me to go.

I really had stayed at the school for as long as I could, and one day the headmaster drove me into Worcester. We stopped near to the cinema, by Worcester Foregate Street station, where I was expected to get out of the car. I remember how he mumbled an apology for leaving me there. He did sound quite upset about abandoning me, and it can't have been easy for him to just leave a child there like that, but he did.

I spent most of the first day wandering around. I didn't know the area, and I had £1.70 in leftover tuck shop money in my pocket. I needed to find somewhere I could leave my suitcase and my few possessions. At the far end of the racetrack I found a place where there were boats for hire and in the evening no one was ever there, so that became a temporary home for me.

I knew I needed to find work, and support myself somehow. I took anything I could, wherever I could get paid without having to declare my address – as I didn't have one. Slowly I took control of my own life, but I didn't know at the time that the worst was still to come.

By now I was known as Vincent Conlan. One day at Croome I had decided that I needed a proper surname and Sister Ursula suggested I choose it from some names she put in a hat. I didn't like the sound of two of these names, but one jumped out at me – Conlon. Another nun suggested I spell it with an 'a', to make it Conlan, and although I didn't realise it at the time, they had guided me into selecting my real name. It wasn't until I saw my birth certificate, aged eighteen, that I discovered it was my mother's maiden name, and I was stunned.

However, having an Irish surname in those days could be problematic. In the early 70s, with the IRA bombings happening in London and around the country, there was an awful lot of anti-Irish sentiment. I suppose I could have changed my name by deed poll and divorced myself from something I had nothing to do with, but I had waited for so long to have my own name that I didn't want to change it.

So for the next few years I lived like a gypsy, always on the move and never staying too long in one place. I would get work wherever I could, which was usually labouring, but basically anywhere that not too many questions were asked. At one point I worked up north in a foundry. I had a motorbike – a 1960's Post Office bike which I had saved up to buy – and I had my freedom, however I was only comfortable staying for as long as it took for someone to hear my surname, and then I would go.

Soon after, I joined the army, and was taken under the wing of a Sergeant Shergold. To me, he seemed like a male version of Sister Ursula, kind and caring. He soon realised that I had come from the care system – probably something to do with the fact that I always made my bed immaculately and kept the dormitory clean! He moved me into a group who all had similar backgrounds to my own.

I now credit Sergeant Shergold with having taught me how society works. He took us out and about, instructing us in life situations, how to socialise, go shopping, find somewhere to live. He was like a father figure to our group, helping us with all things that a parent would normally teach their child. He also taught me how to channel my temper and I took up boxing, as a release for this.

'Hit me,' he would say in the boxing ring, so I did, and he would hit me back. I had a lot of anger bottled up inside me, and would often get into fights, but through his guidance I managed to take control of this.

Finally my life was on a path to normality. Things could have gone in other directions so easily, or I might not have made it at all, had my illness not been dealt with when it was. My childhood and young adulthood hadn't been easy, but now I had my whole life ahead of me, and it was up to me to make the best of any opportunities which came my way. I would make my way in the world. Find a career, love and life.

Finding My Mother

When a child is born, alongside the love from the mother comes a pair of spiritual shoes. They are there, ready for when the child takes his first tentative steps. But if the mother and child are separated for some reason, then one shoe is removed and cast to the far side of the moon.

And so as the child grows up, he walks with a spiritual limp. This tells the world that something terrible has happened, and there is no need for words.

All of my life I lived with this limp, and I spent a large part of my adult life looking for the one person who could cure me of it – my own mother.

Trapped inside that woman is the love she will always have had for her own child, hiding it in her heart. This is the key to returning the spiritual shoe.

At the age of fifty-nine I finally found the one person I had been looking for – my mother. On All

Saints Day, the first day of November, I caught a plane to Shannon airport in Ireland. I landed at 10.30 and at 10.45 I held my mother in my arms. As if by magic, that spiritual shoe found its way onto my foot and I was able to walk without a limp.

I felt complete at last.

My mother passed away in March 2018 with a clean soul.

Sister Ursula

In 2011 I visited St Chad's Cathedral archive department, where I found my school documents.

I put in a request to contact Sister Ursula; I wanted to thank her for her kindness and compassion during my time at the school and tell her what a huge impact she had had on my life. My request to make contact was granted, but I had to send the letter via St Chad's. I sent my letter, but sadly I never had a reply, and I have always wondered if she ever received it.

To this day I have kept something very special with me which belonged to Sister Ursula. Just before I left Croome Court she gave me a rosary. I am sure she wasn't supposed to, but she did, and for many years I kept it hidden. It has always been very precious to me, and I am sure it has kept me safe.

I would like to hope that Sister Ursula was still alive and well when I sent my letter, and that she went to her final resting place knowing just how grateful I was to her.

Photographs

There are very few surviving photographs of me as a child. These were taken between 1967 and 1969.

And this one has a story attached to it. When an archived photo from the 1930s at Besford Court School was accidentally destroyed, I was used as a model to recreate it, as I still had very short hair following my operation.

Results of an MRI Scan in 2001

I n 2001 I received a head injury, following an attempted terrorist attack at work. The following are the results of a scan carried out at that time:

There is quite high tentorium, and extensive collection in midline in the region of the superior vermis and much of the superior and middle vermis is missing. There is some central CSF capacity within the inferior vermis suggestive of central scarring. Cerebellar malacia, hemispheres on either side appear unremarkable in the roofs of the lateral ventricles above the trigones there are high signal areas on T2.

What this means:

The tentorium are membranes in the skull, which enclose different parts of the brain to stabilise it. The ones referred to in this case are at the lower back of the head, where the cerebellum (the part of the brain which coordinates movement) attaches to the brain stem. Here the tentorium is being pushed up – presumably caused by a tumour or abscess near the apex of the cerebellum. Some brain tissue in this area has been destroyed by the tumour and there is excessive brain fluid (CSF = cerebral spinal fluid). The cerebellum is smaller than it should be (malacia) and there is evidence of inflammation. The part of the brain immediately above the tentorium, which is being pushed upwards, is concerned with sight. This could explain why I had poor vision prior to my operation.

It was considered too dangerous for me to return to work and risk any further injury to my head, and so I retired in 2001.

About The Authors

Vincent Conlan

Vincent has had careers in the army, the police, and security services. In 2001 he was caught up in a terrorist attack at work and received a blow to the head. He subsequently retired due to ill health.

Vincent married twice and is now widowed. He lives in Warwickshire, close to his children and grandchildren. In recent years he has devoted himself to tracking down former pupils of St Joseph's School and he manages the Croome Court School Facebook page. He takes an active role in organising annual reunions and exhibitions at the house.

Sara Downing

Sara is the author of five novels. She met Vincent whilst researching her fifth novel, The Lost Boy, which is set at a fictional version of Croome Court. She was captivated by Vincent's story and wove many of his anecdotes into her novel.

Before children, Sara was a Chartered Accountant. She now writes full time and lives in Worcestershire with her husband and three children.

The Lost Boy is available in paperback and eBook from Amazon.

Acknowledgements

From Vincent:

I cannot believe that my story has finally been published. On one hand this is very exciting, but it's also the end of a journey for me.

It's clear from this book that there are certain people to whom I owe a debt of gratitude. Sadly they are no longer around for me to thank, but I hope they went to their final resting places knowing how much good they did.

I would also like to thank Alice Padley and the team at Croome Court for all they do in keeping the spirit of St Joseph's alive. Our reunions mean so much to so many and it has been an honour to be involved. And, of course, Sara, it is thanks to you that my story has now been told. I cannot thank you enough. Bless you, my dear.

From Sara:

Thank you, Vincent, for allowing me to help you tell your story. You are an inspirational man and I hope I have done you proud with this book. Putting myself in your shoes to write it has gone some small way to helping me understand what you went through, and it has been an honour to work with you.

Thanks also go to Richard Lovegrove MB BS MD FRCS(Eng) for the interpretation of Vincent's scan results, and to Alice Padley for introducing me to Vincent in the first place.

Printed in Great Britain
by Amazon